DUETS
in Color
12 Original Duets in Major Keys

Early to Mid-Intermediate

T0081940

Book 1

by Naoko Ikeda

ISBN 978-1-61780-864-7

EXCLUSIVELY DISTRIBUTED BY

WILLIS MUSIC

HAL•LEONARD®
CORPORATION
7777 W. BLUEMOUND RD. P.O. BOX 13819
MILWAUKEE, WISCONSIN 53213

Foreword

I love piano duets, and it has been my dream to write duets in all 24 keys for a long time. I am happy to finally be able to present them to you in these two volumes called *Duets in Color*. Although they are presented separately in major and minor keys, I highly recommend performing them in pairs, e.g. "Coral Sunrise" (C Major) in *Book 1*, and "Silver Rain" (C Minor) in *Book 2*.

We are fortunate to live in a beautiful world that is rich in amazing colors. My sincere hope is that these pieces help you to see them more clearly.

Naoko Ikeda

Biography

Naoko Ikeda lives in Sapporo, Hokkaido in northern Japan. Influenced by classical music, jazz and pop, as well as the piano works of William Gillock, her own music reflects her diverse tastes with beauty, elegance, and humor. Ms. Ikeda holds a piano performance degree from Yamaguchi College of Arts (Japan) and currently maintains an energetic schedule as both teacher and composer.

Contents

4	Coral Sunrise	C Major
10	Vivid Violet	G Major
16	Scarlet Hearts	D Major
23	Emerald Ocean Waves	A Major
28	Yellow Mimosas in Bloom	E Major
33	Blue Skies	B Major
37	Amethyst Stars	F♯ Major
40	Golden Beaches	D♭ Major
45	Pink Topaz	A♭ Major
50	Colorful Reflections	E♭ Major
56	Green Fields in Spring	B♭ Major
60	Magenta Waltz	F Major

Coral Sunrise

Naoko Ikeda

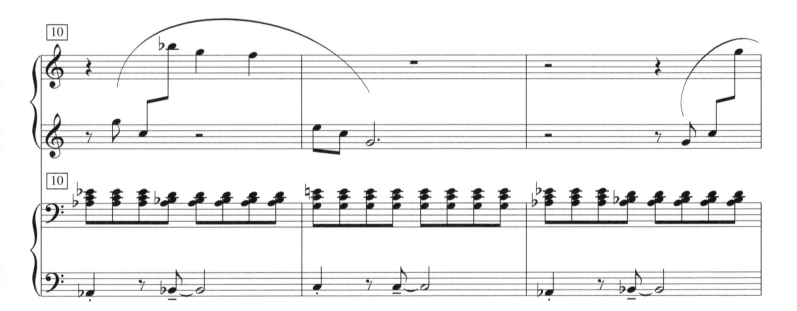

Vivid Violet*

for Sachiko, my sister

Naoko Ikeda

* Previously published as "Sea Breeze."

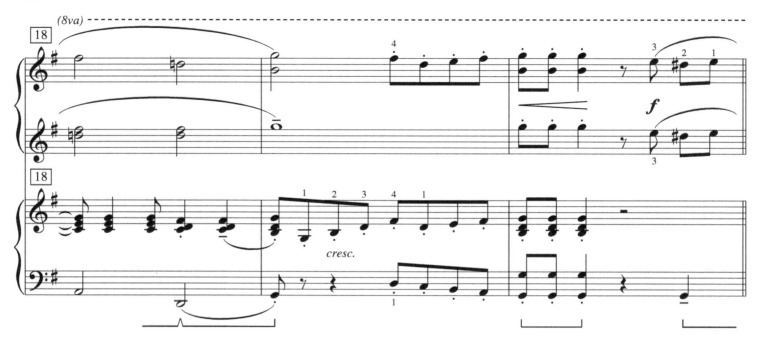

Scarlet Hearts

for Yūki & Shintaro Hasegawa

Naoko Ikeda

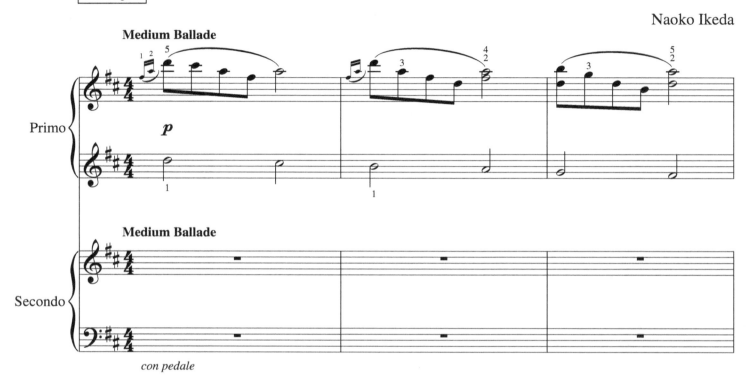

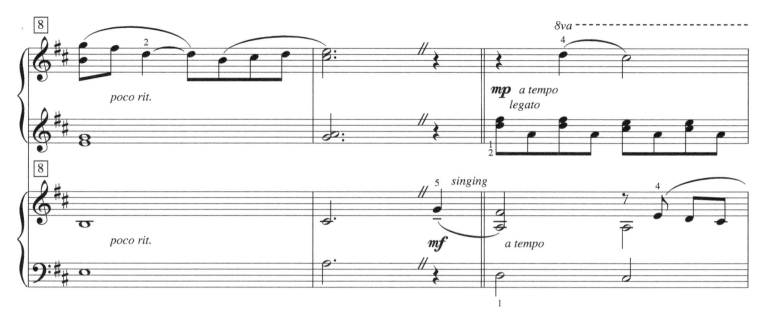

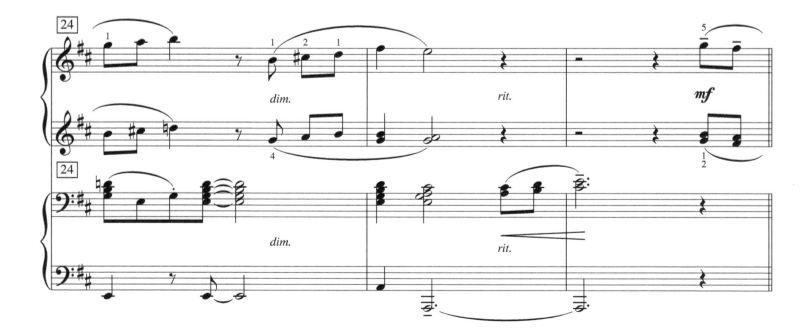

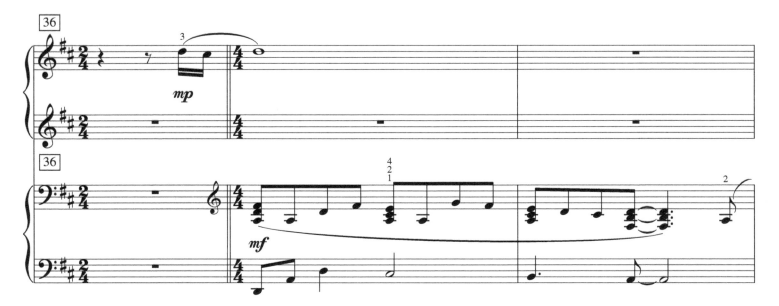

Emerald Ocean Waves

for Teresa Ledford & Charmaine Siagian

Naoko Ikeda

24

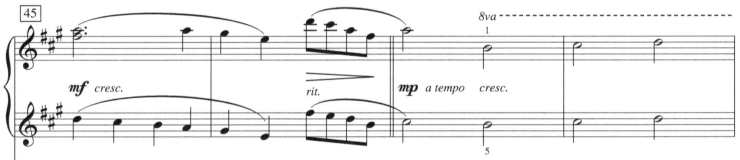

Yellow Mimosas in Bloom

for Shiori & Saya Matsukawa

Naoko Ikeda

E Major

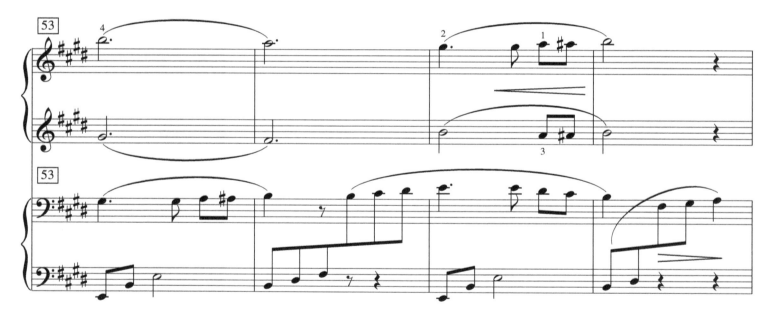

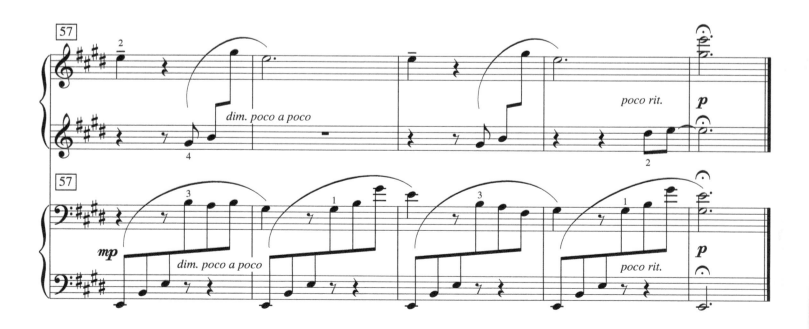

Blue Skies

for Eri, Mari & Haruki Shimatani

Naoko Ikeda

B Major

Amethyst Stars

for Keiko Sakai & Atsuko Hoshino

Naoko Ikeda

Golden Beaches

for Hidenori Uno

Naoko Ikeda

Pink Topaz

for Kaoru Funamizu, Satoko & Mayumi Fujishima

Naoko Ikeda

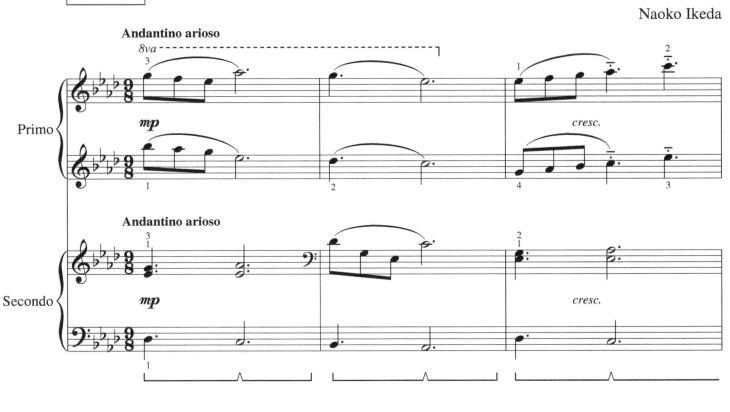

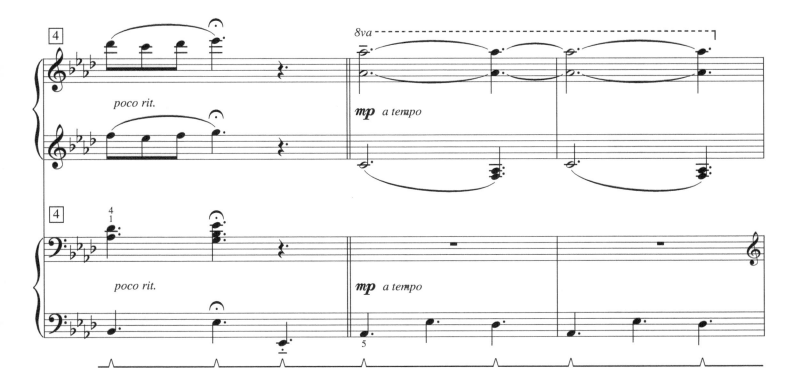

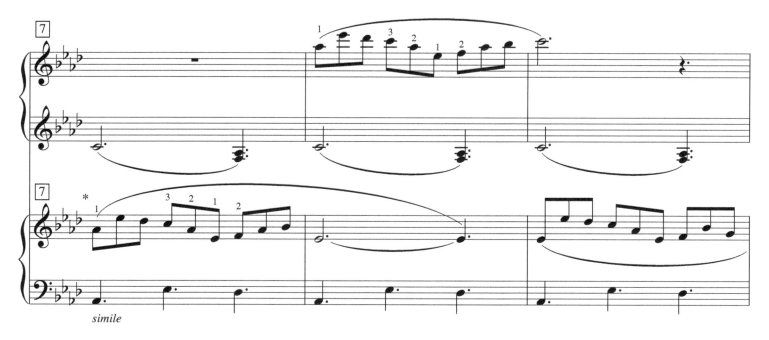

* NOTE: *The right hand of the Secondo plays over (on top of) the left hand of the Primo in mm. 7–14 and mm. 38 to the end.*

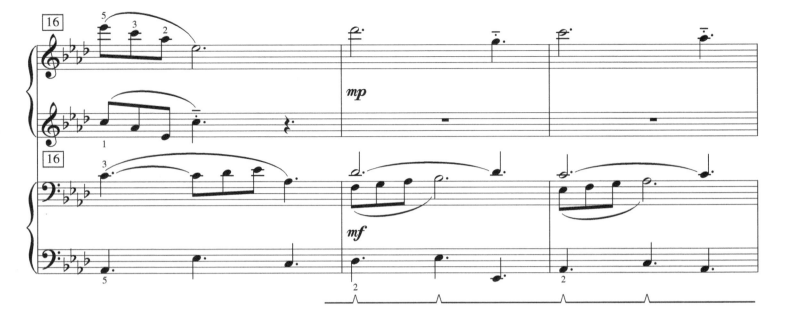

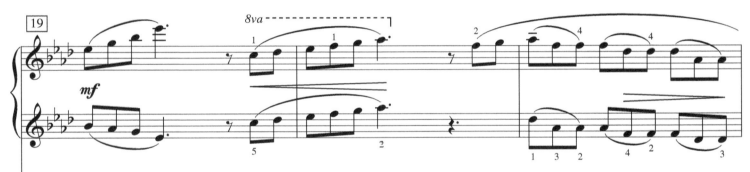

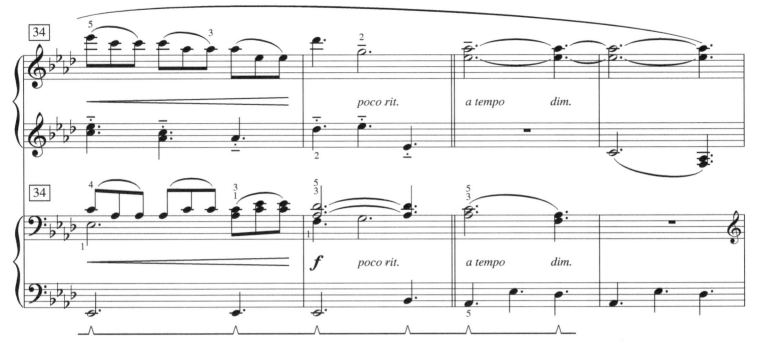

Colorful Reflections

Naoko Ikeda

51

52

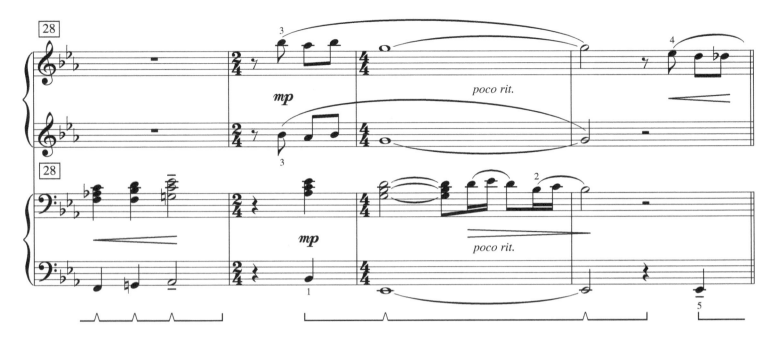

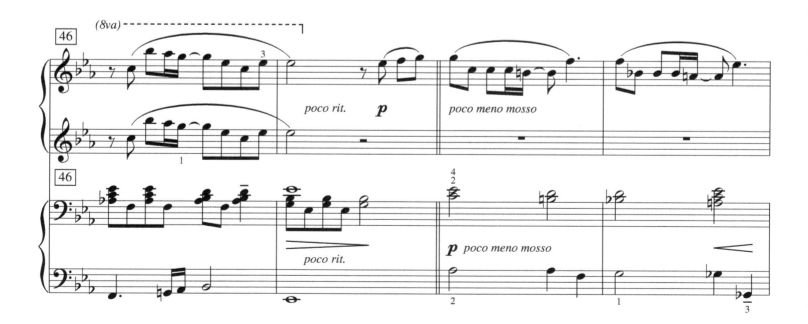

Green Fields in Spring

for Tomomi Nozawa & Michiko Setoda

Naoko Ikeda

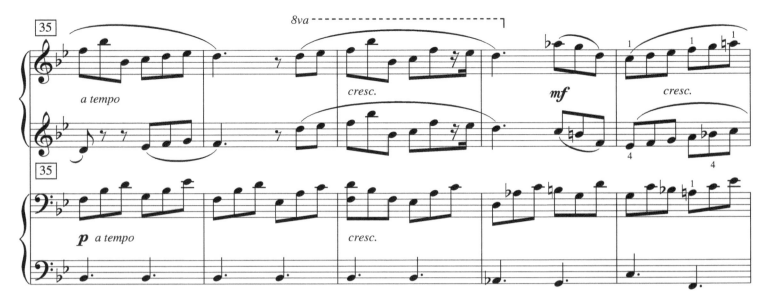

Magenta Waltz*

for Masayo Watanabe

Naoko Ikeda

* Previously published as "Waltz of the Grapes."

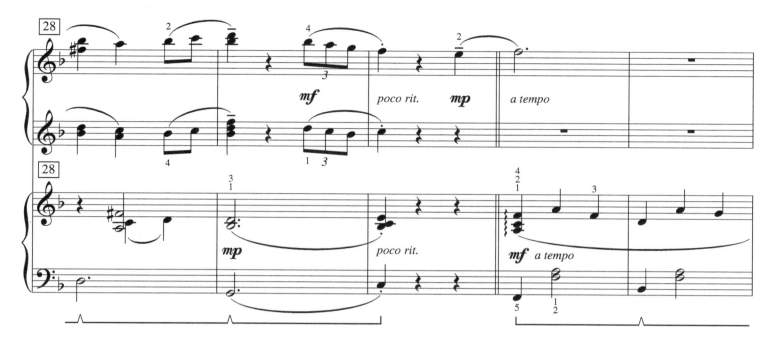

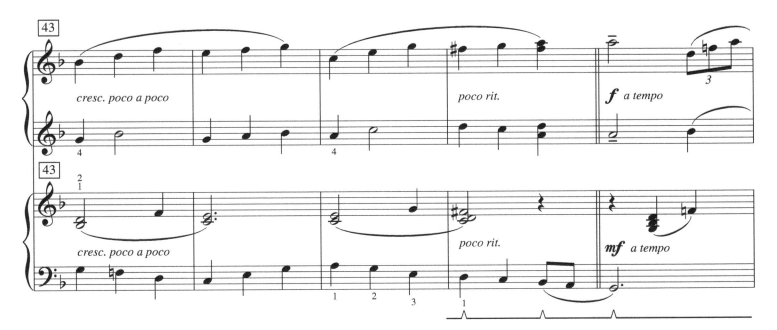

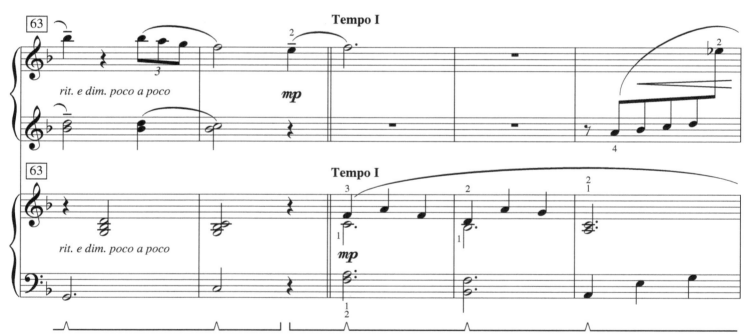

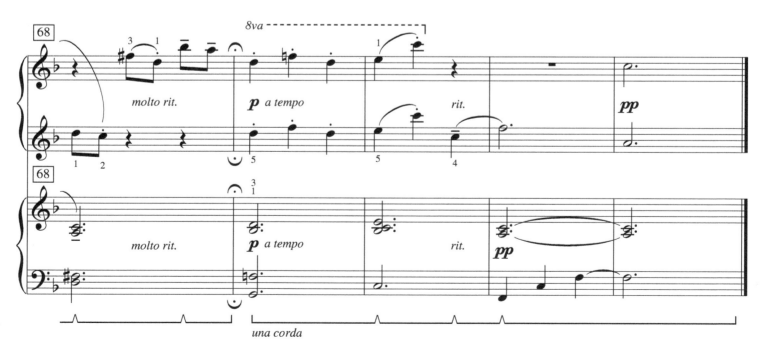